Did Y...

COV...

A MISCELLANY

Compiled by Julia Skinner

With particular reference to the work of David McGrory

THE FRANCIS FRITH COLLECTION

www.francisfrith.com

First published in the United Kingdom in 2008 by The Francis Frith Collection®

Hardback edition published in 2008 ISBN 978-1-84589-389-7

British Library Cataloguing in Publication Data

Did You Know? Coventry - A Miscellany
Compiled by Julia Skinner
With particular reference to the work of David McGrory

The Francis Frith Collection
Frith's Barn, Teffont,
Salisbury, Wiltshire SP3 5QP
Tel: +44 (0) 1722 716 376
Email: info@francisfrith.co.uk
www.francisfrith.com

Printed and bound in Singapore

Front Cover: **COVENTRY, BUTCHER'S ROW 1892** 30916Ap

The colour-tinting is for illustrative purposes only, and is not intended to be historically accurate

CONTENTS

COVENTRY, WHITE FRIARS MONASTERY c1900 C169304

INTRODUCTION

The origins of Coventry are obscure, but in all probability it began in the 7th century with the establishment of a hamlet to serve an Anglo-Saxon convent; both were destroyed by the Danes in 1016. In 1043 Leofric, Earl of Mercia, founded a Benedictine priory which he endowed with half his land in the town - hence the division of the town into the Prior's Half and the Earl's Half. The town itself grew up at the junction of the roads to Warwick, Lichfield, Leicester and London, and its first golden age would dawn during the 14th century. By this time Coventry's trade was founded on wool, leather goods, metal working and the manufacture of soap, but cloth was becoming increasingly important. A poll-tax return for 1377 gives an estimated population of around 7000, making Coventry the fourth town in England after London, Norwich and Bristol. Coventry was seen as a medieval boom town, attracting an influx of people from surrounding villages in search of work.

The Coventry of the 18th century was still dominated by the wool trade, though by 1765 the manufacture of silk ribbons had become a major local industry and would remain so well into the 19th century. The town was also known for watch-making. Coventry's second golden age dawned at the end of the 19th century when it became a major centre for bicycle manufacture - by the mid 1890s there were 80 bicycle firms in and around the town. Further advances came with the rise of motorcycle and motorcar manufacture, and for many years Coventry was the world's biggest car maker.

Coventry for many people is best-known for the terrible destruction it suffered during the Second World War. It endured dozens of air raids from 1940 to 1942, much of the city centre was flattened, and the ancient cathedral church of St Michael was destroyed. It was only in 1962 that the Bishop of Coventry, in the presence of Queen

Elizabeth II, finally consecrated the new, modernist cathedral which replaced it. The gaunt but still splendid ruins of the old building were left to stand, a lasting reminder of the folly of war.

Coventry is now a thriving city, much visited by tourists. It is constantly developing, gaining national awards for its architecture, and is a bustling, multi-cultural city. Coventry, like the phoenix, rose from the ashes, and as it goes forward into the 21st century the phoenix still burns brighter than ever.

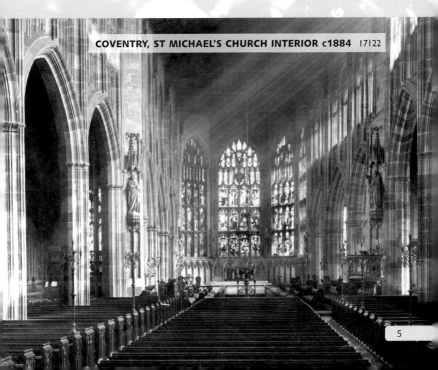

COVENTRY, ST MICHAEL'S CHURCH INTERIOR c1884 17122

COVENTRY WORDS
AND PHRASES

'Batch' - a round bread roll.

'Thrape' - to beat or thrash, as in 'given a thraping' - given a beating.

'Yampy' - mad, daft, barmy.

'Entry' - a passage between houses, or an alleyway.

'Lob' - throw.

'Irked' - annoyed.

'Long seat' - a settee.

'Kaggy-handed' or **'kack-handed'** - left-handed.

'Waggin it' - playing truant, skiving.

'Mardy' - moody, miserable.

'The cut' - the canal.

A 'god cake' is sometimes used in Warwickshire and West Midlands as a name for the triangle of grass at a road junction that is created as the road splits to go left and right. The name refers to the traditional pastry cakes known as Godcakes - see the recipe on page 49.

'Peeping Tom' - the original 'Peeping Tom' of popular legend was a Coventry tailor who disobeyed the command not to watch as Lady Godiva rode naked through the city in an attempt to persuade her husband Earl Leofric to change his mind about increasing local taxes. After taking an illicit peek, Tom was struck blind in a divine act of punishment for his disobedience.

'Coventry True Blue' - in the Middle Ages Coventry was particularly noted for its dark blue dyed thread and cloth, which was so long-lasting that it bore the name 'Coventry True Blue'. The dye is believed to have been made from sloe berries, and the rich dark colour stayed true despite repeated washing, giving rise to the expression 'As true as Coventry Blue'.

'Sent to Coventry' - this phrase means to ignore and not speak to someone. There are several theories about how this phrase came about. The most likely explanation is that it probably derives from the Civil War period, when most of the inhabitants of Coventry supported the Parliamentarian side and the town was considered an ideal place to which to send a large number of Royalist prisoners for safekeeping. It was said that none of the citizens would help the prisoners in any way, and refused to speak to them. The phrase 'Sent to Coventry' thus became a by-word for being completely shunned and ignored.

COVENTRY, RECREATION GROUND 1892 30921

HAUNTED COVENTRY

St Mary's Guildhall is said to be haunted by the ghostly figure of a man in a hooded gown who hovers near the table at official functions.

In olden days a giant black dog with glowing green eyes was believed to roam Whitmore Park at night. Local people avoided the area after dark, as they thought that a sighting of the dog foretold a death in the family.

The Aston Court Hotel in Holyhead Road is said to have a number of ghosts. In April 2003 The Coventry Telegraph reported that a team of paranormal investigators had been called in after strange noises and mysterious events had puzzled the staff. The team concluded there were at least five ghosts in the hotel, two men, two women, and a young girl who they felt was a malevolent spirit - in her lifetime she had been the servant of a man who beat her, and in revenge she now haunts one of the rooms and attacks any men who go in there. Another ghost is of a former cleaner who hides dustpans and other cleaning equipment because she disliked her job so much!

One of the area's most famous haunted buildings is The Phantom Coach public house at Canley, on the A45 Fletchampstead Highway. The pub is named after a coach laden with passengers which plunged off the road and sank in the flooded marshland that then covered the Canley area, killing all on board. The phantom coach is now thought to haunt the area, and several residents have reported hearing the sound of horses galloping past in the night. It is said that on Halloween night the spectral coach can be seen actually traveling through the pub building. The pub is also said to be haunted by the ghost of the coach driver, a mischievous spirit nicknamed Charlie who amuses himself by disconnecting barrels, rattling bottles and hiding things away from the staff. It is said that his presence can be particularly felt in the cellar area.

Coventry is full of other spooky tales - to find out more, read 'Haunted Coventry' by David McGrory (Images of England Series, 2005).

COVENTRY, TRINITY CHURCH
1892 30927

COVENTRY, BUTCHER'S ROW 1892 30916a

**COVENTRY, THE PARISH
CHURCH c1965** C169126

12

COVENTRY MISCELLANY

In 1947 a Bronze Age axe-head was unearthed in Broadgate dating to 650BC.

The earliest spelling of Coventry is 'Couaentree' and not Cofantreo, as is often claimed.

A hoard of Roman coins was found at Bullester Fields Farm, Foleshill on 17 December 1793.

Henry IV held the Unlearned Parliament (or Lack Learning Parliament, because of the absence of lawyers) in Coventry in 1404 to try to raise revenue from the church. He was unsuccessful.

After failing to get permission to walk the high wire between Holy Trinity and St Michael, in 1884 Charles Blondin walked the high wire over Quinton Pool, stopping halfway to stand on his head.

Stivichall Church is reputed to have been built by one stonemason and one labourer.

During the First World War the ordnance factory in Red Lane produced 15 and 18-inch naval guns which were tested in a pit on site.

Originally the columns in the new cathedral were supposed to have rested upon glass balls.

Sir Thomas More visited his sister in Coventry on more than one occasion. She was married to writer of plays and pageants William Rastell who died in prison in 1536.

COVENTRY, ST MARY'S HALL 1892 30929

15

COVENTRY, ST MICHAEL'S CHURCH 1892 30922

Part of the carpet used in Westminster Abbey during Queen Elizabeth II's coronation can be seen by the altar in Holy Trinity Church.

Parts of the Coventry Mystery Plays were rehearsed in St Mary's Hall.

COVENTRY, ST MARY'S HALL INTERIOR 1892 30931

Air raid shelters began to be constructed in Coventry in September 1938, a year before the war started.

Thomas Loseby the creator of the old Market Hall Clock, which today still powers the Godiva Clock, agreed to be fined £1 for every minute it lost.

During the Wars of the Roses (fought between 1455 to 1487) Henry VI moved his entire royal court to Coventry and based it here for 2½ to 3 years.

On 15 December 1857 Charles Dickens read his 'Christmas Carol' in the Corn Exchange in Hertford Street.

Henry VIII was the last royal visitor to Coventry Priory in 1509, bringing with him his then queen, Catherine of Aragon.

COVENTRY, FORD'S HOSPITAL 1892 30917

COVENTRY, THE BLUE COAT SCHOOL
c1890 C169301

Lady Godiva's real name was Godgifu, pronounced Godgivu and meaning God's Gift.

The priory church of St Mary, dissolved in 1539 by Henry VIII, measured a massive 425 feet long.

In the late 19th century local clergy and some local citizens tried to ban the Godiva Processions, claiming that they were indecent.

In New Union Street at the entrance to Cheylesmore gatehouse can be seen the only cannon bollards in Coventry, made from real cannons.

Although not recorded in the City Annals, Oliver Cromwell came to Coventry on at least three occasions.

Edward III held a joust in Coventry in which he wore a borrowed suit of rare, 'studded' armour, which belonged to Sir Thomas Bradstone.

Sir Roger Mortimer, the lover of Queen Isabella (wife of Edward II), was buried in Coventry Greyfriars church after his death in 1330. It is said he may have been moved but no record of his removal exists.

COVENTRY, SWANSWELL PARK c1955 C169016

COVENTRY, HERTFORD STREET c1955 C169006

Recently an Iron Age settlement of roundhouses was discovered near Gibbet Hill while laying out a sports pitch at the University of Warwick.

Whitley Common was the main scene of all hangings in Coventry from the late-17th to mid-19th century. The last person to hang there was Mary Ann Higgins on 11 August 1831.

The old Whitefriars monastery, when it belonged to the Hales family and was known as 'Hales Place', saw some important visitors, the most important being Queen Elizabeth I, Mary, Queen of Scots and her son James I.

James II held mass in Palace Yard, a 15th-century mansion, which up until the war stood opposite the Council House. The tapestries which decorated the dining room in which he dined, can still be seen in St Mary's Hall.

COVENTRY, FORD'S HOSPITAL 1892 30918

Did You Know?
COVENTRY
A MISCELLANY

COVENTRY, THE CATHEDRAL RUINS c1955 C169012

The King's Window and the Coventry Tapestry in St Mary's Hall are the last major vestiges of the veneration of Henry VI as a saint in England.

Coventry old cathedral was destroyed on the night of 14/15 November 1940 by incendiary bombs which took hold in the roof space of the north aisle.

King Charles I tried in August 1642 to start the Civil War from walled Coventry, but being repulsed he raised the royal standard in Nottingham instead.

Local legend claims that the Roman general Julius Agricola built a camp on Barr's Hill. Coins and pottery found there in the past seem to back up the legend.

Andrew Ernest Stoddart, captain of the Victorian Ashes-winning England cricket team in 1894-5 and John George Wood, England's most popular Victorian naturalist, are both buried in the small churchyard at Radford.

Lady Godiva is not buried in Coventry as many have claimed, but she lies in the now gone Evesham Abbey, buried next to her father confessor.

The first war memorial erected after the First World War was in the village of Radford, paid for by Vernon Pugh of Radford House, director of the Rudge Cycle Company.

The church of the Greyfriars was destroyed during the Dissolution leaving only the tower and spire. It was later used as a pigsty and was styled the tallest pigsty in England. It was rebuilt in 1830-2, but again destroyed by bombs during the Second World War, leaving once more only the tower and spire.

COVENTRY, ST MARY'S HALL,
COURTYARD 1892 30930

COVENTRY, GREYFRIARS GREEN c1955 C169007

ASHOW, CHURCH AND BRIDGE 1892 30996

It is now known that William Shakespeare played St Mary's Hall at least six times.

Broadgate is so named because Hugh Keviloc, Earl of Chester, refers to the 'Broad Gate' of his castle in a late12th-century boundary charter, 'lata porta mei castelli.'

Earl Marmion of Tamworth attacked Coventry Castle in 1143 and was decapitated in his own defensive ditches. Another to attack the castle was one Richard de Lucy who placed it under siege in 1173.

The State Chair in St Mary's Hall probably originated as the bishop's throne from Coventry Priory. The late 14th-century chair was brought into the hall after the Dissolution and is one of the best in England.

COVENTRY, THREE SPIRES c1890 C169002

During the late 19th century Coventry became the biggest maker of bicycles in the world.

A E Mason the author of 'The Three Feathers' was Liberal MP for Coventry from 1906 to 1910. He based part of his novel 'The Turnstile' on Coventry.

Coventry's Transport Museum houses the two fastest cars in the world, 'Thrust 2' and 'Thrust SSC'.

Best-selling author of 'jolly hockey sticks' girls' story books Angela Brazil lived with her brother Walter and sister Amy at No. 1, The Quadrant.

In 1855 William Makepeace Thackeray stayed with George Eliot's friends the Brays at Rosehill in Radford. It is recorded that while there he wrote part of his novel 'The Newcomes'.

COVENTRY, THE CATHEDRAL AND HOLY TRINITY c1955 C169502

COVENTRY, THE LADY GODIVA CLOCK c1965 C169026

Did You Know?
COVENTRY
A MISCELLANY

In March 1772 Mary Clues of Gosford Street was consumed by fire in a rare case of apparent spontaneous human combustion.

On 12 June 1849 William Wombell of Wombell's Menagerie was killed by one of his own elephants at Coventry Fair. His grave can still be seen in the London Road Cemetery.

COVENTRY, BROADGATE c1955 C169023

The tapestry hanging behind the High Altar in Coventry Cathedral is said to be the biggest in the world. Roughly the size of a tennis court, it was created by Graham Sutherland, inspired by the Biblical Book of Revelation.

Coventry clockmaker Samuel Watson was appointed Mathematician in Ordinary to Charles II and to Queen Mary. Watson clocks were unusual because they displayed the full motions of the planets.

COVENTRY, ST JOHN'S HOSPITAL 1892 30919

38

**COVENTRY, HIGH STREET AND
BROADGATE c1955** C169003

**COVENTRY, ST JOHN'S
CHURCH c1884** 17127

COVENTRY, THE PRECINCT c1965 C169020

Coventry's pedestrian precinct was the first of its kind in the world and has since been copied the world over.

The 15th-century oak armoured figure in Cathedral Lane which has been used to represent Peeping Tom since the 17th century probably actually portrays St George. It is most likely that it originated from Coventry Priory, where a relic of St George was kept.

COVENTRY, CROSS CHEAPING 1892 30914

SPORTING COVENTRY

Coventry City Football Club was founded in 1883 by employees of the Singers cycle firm, hence the club's first nickname of 'The Singers'. The club is now known as 'The Sky Blues'. Coventry City FC suffered the worst ever defeat in the club's history in 1901, losing 11-2 against Berwick Rangers in the qualifying round of the FA Cup, but made up for it in 1987 when the team brought the FA Cup home after winning 3-2 against Tottenham Hotspur in a memorable final at Wembley. This was a notable year for local football fans, as Coventry also won the FA Youth Cup in 1987. Coventry City FC were promoted to Division One in 1967 under the legendary management of Jimmy Hill, who also co-wrote the club song, the Sky Blue anthem, which is sung to the tune of the Eton Boating Song. Coventry City FC were founder members of the Premier League in 1992, but were relegated in 2001 and currently play in the Coca-Coca Championship.

Coventry is also home to several more unusual sporting teams. Coventry Blaze is a successful British ice hockey team and won the Elite Ice Hockey League Championship for the third time in four years in 2008. The Coventry Cassidy Jets are an American Football team, they won the BAFL Division 2 Championship in 2005 and were undefeated all season.

Also in Coventry's sporting hall of fame are the Coventry Bees motorcycle speedway team. They won the British Elite League Speedway Championship in 2007, making this the eighth time that the club have been crowned League Champions. In 2007 the Bees also won the Elite League Knockout Cup for the third time in their history, as well as the Craven Shield.

Coventry has an impressive list of people born in the city who have gone on to sporting success, including David Moorcroft, a 1500m and 5000m runner whose career spanned the late 1970s and early 1980s. Moorcroft attended Woodlands School and was a member of the Coventry Godiva Harriers athletics club. He won gold in the 1500m in the 1978 Commonwealth Games, and a further gold in the 5000m at the 1982 Commonwealth Games. Another athletics star who hails from Coventry is the Olympic gold medalist Marlon Devenish, also a member of the Coventry Godiva Harriers athletics club. Devenish won his medal in the 2004 Olympics in a thrilling 4 x 100m relay final, along with Jason Gardener, Darren Campbell and Mark Lewis-Francis, when the quartet spectacularly defeated the race favourites, the United States team, by just 0.01 seconds.

Ian Bell is a Coventry-born England Test cricketer who plays county cricket for Warwickshire County Cricket Club. He was part of the team which won the Ashes for England in 2005.

Two members of the 2003 Rugby Union World Cup winning squad were Coventry-born, Danny Grewock and Neil Black. Danny Grewock attended Woodlands School and played for the Warwickshire U21 side at the age of 19, playing for England for the first time in 1997. He could only make one appearance during the 2003 Rugby World Cup because of a hand injury early on the tournament. His England team-mate and fellow Coventrarian Neil Black has captained both England and Leicester in a career in which he has gained 66 caps for England. He also attended Woodlands School and represented England at U18, U21 and 'A' level, then made his full England debut in 1994. He scored several tries in the 2003 Rugby World Cup tournament.

QUIZ QUESTIONS

Answers on page 50.

1. A lead figure of Lady Godiva can be seen in Trinity Street - where exactly can she be found?

2. Holy Trinity Church in Coventry contains one of the nation's best examples of what?

3. Who was the world-famous novelist who attended the school of the Franklin sisters at the end of Warwick Row?

4. Where was arguably the first British-built motorcar constructed?

5. What dubious place in Coventry's history is held by Mary Ball?

6. What was the original name of the River Sherbourne?

7. Where did the material for the font of the new Coventry Cathedral come from?

8. What feat of skill did Ramon Kelvik perform in Coventry city centre on the night of December 31st 1999, to mark the new millennium?

9. Where in Coventry can you find the Shakespeare Table, and what is its supposed connection with the Bard?

10. Who is commemorated by the Whittle Arch, the huge sculpture in Millennium Place?

COVENTRY, STATUE OF LADY GODIVA c1900 C169303

RECIPE

WARWICKSHIRE STEW

This recipe reflects the fact that Coventry was in Warwickshire until the Local Government Act of 1972, which came into effect in 1974. This dish is a way of cooking the tougher beef cuts gently and slowly.

Ingredients

675g/1½ lb stewing steak
2 tablespoonfuls seasoned plain flour
1 tablespoonful oil or beef dripping
150ml/5fl oz beef stock or red wine
6 potatoes, diced
4 carrots, diced
2 onions, cut into quarters
350g/12oz tomatoes
110g/4oz mushrooms, cut into quarters
2 cloves garlic, crushed
1 tablespoonful chopped parsley
Salt and pepper

Pre-heat the oven to 140°C/275°F/Gas Mark 1.

Cut the beef into cubes, and lightly dust with seasoned flour. Heat the oil in a frying pan and fry the beef cubes in batches, to seal and colour the meat. Remove the meat from the pan and place in a casserole dish, then add the stock or wine to the frying pan and heat gently, stirring all the time and making sure to scrape the bottom of the pan to collect all the flour. Add all the remaining ingredients to the casserole dish and pour over the warmed stock or wine. Cover and cook for about 5-6 hours.

RECIPE

COVENTRY GODCAKES

These cakes were traditionally given by godparents in the Coventry area to their godchildren on New Year's Eve, for good luck. The child received both a blessing and a cake from the godparent, but the size of the cakes could vary, depending on the wealth and generosity of the giver!

Ingredients

225g/8oz puff pastry (ready-made is fine)
110g/4oz mincemeat
1 egg white, beaten

2 teaspoonfuls rum or brandy (optional)
Caster sugar

Pre-heat the oven to 220°C/425°F/Gas Mark 7.

Roll out the pastry thinly on a lightly floured surface. Cut the pastry into 10cm (4 inch) squares, then cut each square in half on the diagonal to produce two triangles.

Mix the mincemeat with the rum or brandy if used, then place a small spoonful of mincemeat in the middle of half the pastry triangles - don't be too generous with the mixture or it will spill out from the sides of the cakes when the 'lids' are added.

Moisten the edges of the triangles with a little water, then cover each filled triangle with a second triangle on top, pressing down firmly to seal the edges.

Cut three small diagonal slashes across the top of each Godcake with a sharp knife (some traditions say that these represent the Holy Trinity), then brush the top of each cake with beaten egg white and sprinkle with caster sugar. Place the Godcakes on a greased baking sheet and bake for about 15 minutes, or until golden and well puffed up.

Cool on a wire rack and eat as soon as possible!

Did You Know?
COVENTRY
A MISCELLANY

QUIZ ANSWERS

1. A figure of Lady Godiva can be seen cast in lead on the Flying Standard pub.

2. A Doom Painting. This work of art in Holy Trinity Church, only uncovered and restored in recent years, is described as 'one of the most important discoveries ever made in the field of medieval art'. It is believed that the Doom (a depiction of Judgement Day) was painted around 1435, a few years after an earthquake had shaken Coventry.

3. Mary Ann Evans, better known as the author George Eliot, attended the Franklins' school in Warwick Row in Coventry between 1832 and 1835 (the school building still exists; it was later called Nantglyn, and now houses an estate agent). She later came to live with her father in a house later called 'Bird Grove' off the Foleshill Road, and part of the house still exists, although it is now used as an evangelical church which can be seen from George Eliot Road. Coventry is believed to be the model for the town in George Eliot's novel 'Middlemarch', and the author based Hetty Sorrel's trial scene in 'Adam Bede' in St Mary's Hall in Coventry. As the hall was sometimes used as a court of justice she had probably attended a trial here.

4. Motor Mills in Draper's Field, Radford, off Sandy Lane. It had previously been a cotton mill. The inventor of the safety cycle, Harry Lawson, set up a factory at the mill, which was shared with Daimler and other companies, and in 1896 he started the Great Horseless Carriage Company there. While Daimler initially built engines, the GHCC produced British versions of the Boulee tricar. Francis Bacon, works manager of the company, later said that

the GHCC built its own design of vehicle with a Daimler engine, one of which was supplied to Lord Iveagh for the Duke of York. Baron said that this vehicle was finished in June 1897, almost two months before the first Daimler-built car was completed, whose proving run took place in October 1897. Baron wrote of the first car in the 'Autocar' magazine: 'I contend that that car I have mentioned, which worked continuously without the slightest hitch, being the first petrol car built in England, contributed as much to the present motor industry as George Stephenson's first locomotive to railway development.'

5. Mary Ball was the last person to be executed by hanging in Coventry. She was hanged before thousands of spectators outside Coventry Gaol on 9th August 1849 for the crime of poisoning her husband in Nuneaton.

6. The River Cune.

7. The font is cut into a boulder which was brought from Bethlehem.

8. The French high-wire performance artist Ramon Kelvik walked a tightrope between the towers of Holy Trinity Church and St Michael's Church as the 20th century gave way to the 21st.

9. The Shakespeare Table is in the Old Council Chamber in St Mary's Hall. It was sold to the city over 100 years ago by Lord Lucy, who claimed that it was the table on which the warrant was signed for the arrest of William Shakespeare as a young man, for the crime of deer poaching.

10. The Whittle Arch commemorates Frank Whittle, the inventor of the jet engine, who was born in 1907 in Newcome Road, Earlsdon - one of Coventry's world-changing sons.

COVENTRY, HIGH STREET c1955 C169010

FRANCIS FRITH

PIONEER VICTORIAN PHOTOGRAPHER

Francis Frith, founder of the world-famous photographic archive, was a complex and multi-talented man. A devout Quaker and a highly successful Victorian businessman, he was philosophical by nature and pioneering in outlook. By 1855 he had already established a wholesale grocery business in Liverpool, and sold it for the astonishing sum of £200,000, which is the equivalent today of over £15,000,000. Now in his thirties, and captivated by the new science of photography, Frith set out on a series of pioneering journeys up the Nile and to the Near East.

INTRIGUE AND EXPLORATION

He was the first photographer to venture beyond the sixth cataract of the Nile. Africa was still the mysterious 'Dark Continent', and Stanley and Livingstone's historic meeting was a decade into the future. The conditions for picture taking confound belief. He laboured for hours in his wicker dark-room in the sweltering heat of the desert, while the volatile chemicals fizzed dangerously in their trays. Back in London he exhibited his photographs and was 'rapturously cheered' by members of the Royal Society. His reputation as a photographer was made overnight.

VENTURE OF A LIFE-TIME

By the 1870s the railways had threaded their way across the country, and Bank Holidays and half-day Saturdays had been made obligatory by Act of Parliament. All of a sudden the working man and his family were able to enjoy days out, take holidays, and see a little more of the world.

With typical business acumen, Francis Frith foresaw that these new tourists would enjoy having souvenirs to commemorate their days out. For the next thirty years he travelled the country by train and by pony and trap, producing fine photographs of seaside resorts and beauty spots that were keenly bought by millions of Victorians. These prints were painstakingly pasted into family albums and pored over during the dark nights of winter, rekindling precious memories of summer excursions. Frith's studio was soon supplying retail shops all over the country, and by 1890 F Frith & Co had become the greatest specialist photographic publishing company in the world, with over 2,000 sales outlets, and pioneered the picture postcard.

FRANCIS FRITH'S LEGACY

Francis Frith had died in 1898 at his villa in Cannes, his great project still growing. By 1970 the archive he created contained over a third of a million pictures showing 7,000 British towns and villages.

Frith's legacy to us today is of immense significance and value, for the magnificent archive of evocative photographs he created provides a unique record of change in the cities, towns and villages throughout Britain over a century and more. Frith and his fellow studio photographers revisited locations many times down the years to update their views, compiling for us an enthralling and colourful pageant of British life and character.

We are fortunate that Frith was dedicated to recording the minutiae of everyday life. For it is this sheer wealth of visual data, the painstaking chronicle of changes in dress, transport, street layouts, buildings, housing and landscape that captivates us so much today, offering us a powerful link with the past and with the lives of our ancestors.

Computers have now made it possible for Frith's many thousands of images to be accessed almost instantly. The archive offers every one of us an opportunity to examine the places where we and our families have lived and worked down the years. Its images, depicting our shared past, are now bringing pleasure and enlightenment to millions around the world a century and more after his death.

For further information visit: www.francisfrith.com

INTERIOR DECORATION

Frith's photographs can be seen framed and as giant wall murals in thousands of pubs, restaurants, hotels, banks, retail stores and other public buildings throughout Britain. These provide interesting and attractive décor, generating strong local interest and acting as a powerful reminder of gentler days in our increasingly busy and frenetic world.

FRITH PRODUCTS

All Frith photographs are available as prints and posters in a variety of different sizes and styles. In the UK we also offer a range of other gift and stationery products illustrated with Frith photographs, although many of these are not available for delivery outside the UK – see our web site for more information on the products available for delivery in your country.

THE INTERNET

Over 100,000 photographs of Britain can be viewed and purchased on the Frith web site. The web site also includes memories and reminiscences contributed by our customers, who have personal knowledge of localities and of the people and properties depicted in Frith photographs. If you wish to learn more about a specific town or village you may find these reminiscences fascinating to browse. Why not add your own comments if you think they would be of interest to others? See **www.francisfrith.com**

PLEASE HELP US BRING FRITH'S PHOTOGRAPHS TO LIFE

Our authors do their best to recount the history of the places they write about. They give insights into how particular towns and villages developed, they describe the architecture of streets and buildings, and they discuss the lives of famous people who lived there. But however knowledgeable our authors are, the story they tell is necessarily incomplete.

Frith's photographs are so much more than plain historical documents. They are living proofs of the flow of human life down the generations. They show real people at real moments in history; and each of those people is the son or daughter of someone, the brother or sister, aunt or uncle, grandfather or grandmother of someone else. All of them lived, worked and played in the streets depicted in Frith's photographs.

We would be grateful if you would give us your insights into the places shown in our photographs: the streets and buildings, the shops, businesses and industries. Post your memories of life in those streets on the Frith website: what it was like growing up there, who ran the local shop and what shopping was like years ago; if your workplace is shown tell us about your working day and what the building is used for now. Read other visitors' memories and reconnect with your shared local history and heritage. With your help more and more Frith photographs can be brought to life, and vital memories preserved for posterity, and for the benefit of historians in the future.

Wherever possible, we will try to include some of your comments in future editions of our books. Moreover, if you spot errors in dates, titles or other facts, please let us know, because our archive records are not always completely accurate—they rely on 140 years of human endeavour and hand-compiled records. You can email us using the contact form on the website.

Thank you!

For further information, trade, or author enquiries
please contact us at the address below:

The Francis Frith Collection, Frith's Barn, Teffont, Salisbury, Wiltshire, England SP3 5QP.

Tel: +44 (0)1722 716 376 Fax: +44 (0)1722 716 881
e-mail: sales@francisfrith.co.uk **www.francisfrith.com**